BALANCING ACT

A Teen's Guide to Managing Stress

The Science of Health: Youth and Well-Being

BALANCING ACT

A Teen's Guide to Managing Stress

by Joan Esherick

Mason Crest Publishers

Philadelphia

Mason Crest Publishers Inc.
370 Reed Road, Broomall, Pennsylvania 19008
(866) MCP-BOOK (toll free)
www.masoncrest.com

ISBN 1-59084-840-3 (series)

Library of Congress Cataloging-in-Publication Data

Esherick, Joan.
  Balancing act : a teen's guide to managing stress / by Joan Esherick.
     p. cm. — (The science of health : youth and well-being)
  Includes bibliographical references and index.
  ISBN 1-59084-853-5
  1. Stress management for teenagers—Juvenile literature. I. Title. II.
Science of health.
  RA785.E83 2004
  155.5'18—dc22
                          2004010693

First edition, 2005
13 12 11 10 09 08 07 06 05   10 9 8 7 6 5 4 3 2

Designed and produced by Harding House Publishing Service,
Vestal, NY 13850.
Cover design by Benjamin Stewart and Michelle Bouch.
Printed and bound in India.

This book is meant to educate and should not be used as an alternative to appropriate medical care. Its creators have made every effort
to ensure that the information presented is accurate and up to
date—but this book is not intended to substitute for the help and
services of trained medical professionals.

CONTENTS

INTRODUCTION
by Dr. Sara Forman

You're not a little kid anymore. When you look in the mirror, you probably see a new person, someone who's taller, bigger, with a face that's starting to look more like an adult's than a child's. And the changes you're experiencing on the inside may be even more intense than the ones you see in the mirror. Your emotions are changing, your attitudes are changing, and even the way you think is changing. Your friends are probably more important to you than they used to be, and you no longer expect your parents to make all your decisions for you. You may be asking more questions and posing more challenges to the adults in your life. You might experiment with new identities—new ways of dressing, hairstyles, ways of talking—as you try to determine just who you really are. Your body is maturing sexually, giving you a whole new set of confusing and exciting feelings. Sorting out what is right and wrong for you may seem overwhelming.

Growth and development during adolescence is a multifaceted process involving every aspect of your being. It all happens so fast that it can be confusing and distressing. But this stage of your life is entirely normal. Every adult in your life made it through adolescence—and you will too.

7

Balancing Act

But what exactly is adolescence? According to the American Heritage Dictionary, adolescence is "the period of physical and psychological development from the onset of puberty to maturity." What does this really mean?

In essence, adolescence is the time in our lives when the needs of childhood give way to the responsibilities of adulthood. According to psychologist Erik Erikson, these years are a time of separation and individuation. In other words, you are separating from your parents, becoming an individual in your own right. These are the years when you begin to make decisions on your own. You are becoming more self-reliant and less dependent on family members.

When medical professionals look at what's happening physically—what they refer to as the biological model— they define the teen years as a period of hormonal transformation toward sexual maturity, as well as a time of peak growth, second only to the growth during the months of infancy. This physical transformation from childhood to adulthood takes place under the influence of society's norms and social pressures; at the same time your body is changing, the people around you are expecting new things from you. This is what makes adolescence such a unique and challenging time.

Being a teenager in North America today is exciting yet stressful. For those who work with teens, whether by parenting them, educating them, or providing services to them, adolescence can be challenging as well. Youth are struggling with many messages from society and the media about how they should behave and who they should be. "Am I normal?" and "How do I fit in?" are often questions with which teens wrestle. They are facing decisions about their health such as how to take care of their bodies, whether to use drugs and alcohol, or whether to have sex.

This series of books on adolescents' health issues provides teens, their parents, their teachers, and all those who work with them accurate information and the tools to keep them safe and healthy. The topics include information about:

- normal growth
- social pressures
- emotional issues
- specific diseases to which adolescents are prone
- stressors facing youth today
- sexuality

The series is a dynamic set of books, which can be shared by youth and the adults who care for them. By providing this information to educate in these areas, these books will help build a foundation for readers so they can begin to work on improving the health and well-being of youth today.

1

STRESSED TO THE MAX:
Teens Under Pressure

Dirk (age 12): *I can't believe they're really gonna do it. I mean, like, I never thought they'd use the "D" word. When Mom and Dad told me and Ryan to come into the living room, I knew something was up. I could tell by the tone of*

Balancing Act

Dad's voice when he said we had to have a family meeting. I hate family meetings. They're always about something serious or stupid. I thought we were in trouble, like maybe we were gonna get the lecture about leaving the PS2 hooked up to the TV again or that we were gonna get the talk on "appropriate Internet use," but I never in a million years expected this. I can't believe it. Mom and Dad want a divorce! A DIVORCE! What am I supposed to do with that? Yeah, they fight a lot. I wish they wouldn't. But split up? How come? What did I do wrong? What are me and Ryan supposed to do? Where are we gonna live? Are we gonna have to change schools? What about my friends? What about the soccer team? How can I stay on the team if I have to live in two places? Ryan started to cry; he's just a little kid. I didn't. I'm just really mad!

Missy (age 14): *I can't believe I made the squad!!! Me! A cheerleader! I thought those girls hated me. I felt like such a klutz when I tried out. I even messed up the back handspring, and I forgot part of one cheer. I was so nervous I thought I was going to puke. I was sure I got cut. But I made it! I really made it! I can't wait till the first game. The new uniforms look so good! When I wear mine to school, I just know Joey will notice me. He HAS to. I'll just die if he doesn't. But what if he doesn't? What if I don't fit in? The other cheerleaders are so cool. What if they don't accept me?*

Angeline (age 13): *Mr. Rodriguez hates me. I just know it. Every time I ask a question in class he disses me. He makes that funny clucking noise with his tongue and says the answer is obvious. Not to me it's not. And then he says in that sarcastic little voice of his, "Can anyone help Miss Cortez with her question?" I feel so humiliated. I'm the stupidest one in the class, I'll admit it, but he doesn't have to put me*

13

down. I mean, like, I'm really trying. I spent more than eight hours on that last diagram—eight whole hours—and just because I can't draw he gives me a D+! I really worked hard on that. It's not fair. I just know I'm going to fail tomorrow's test. I studied. I really did, and I know the stuff, but I'm so nervous around him that I can't remember anything. I may as well quit trying. I'm stupid. I'll never be anything else. Why bother? Every time I think about taking this test tomorrow I feel sick.

Lauren (age 15): *Oh m'gosh! I'm in trouble. I promised Adrian I'd go to his prom with him, but my lacrosse team made district finals. And, of course, the finals have to be on the same day as Central's prom. They're so stupid; why do schools plan stuff this way? I can't tell Coach I can't play—she'll kick me off the team, and I just can't tell Adrian I can't go—he'll hate me forever. What am I going to do? Maybe we can go late to the prom. Maybe we can skip the dinner thing. But I still won't have time to get my hair done. Oh, man. I guess I have to cancel my appointment. I don't know what to do.*

Jessie (age 16): *Anybody know where I can get some fast cash? Zach's youth group is going snowboarding this weekend and I really want to go, but I'm broke. I'm always broke. Between gas for the car, car insurance, clothes, and doing stuff with friends, I never have any money. Working minimum wage doesn't help, even twenty-five hours a week. With school I don't have time for more hours, but I need the money. I'm not one of those rich girls whose daddies hand them everything. Nope, not me. Since the old man split, it's just me and my mom. She works hard, but she can't afford to give me money, so it's up to me. What I do, I have to pay for. That's just the way it is. I tried selling some of my CDs to the kid I baby-sit for. No deal. Maybe*

Balancing Act

I'll just have to work some longer hours this week. But I'm so tired already. Guess I'll just have to suck it up.

Matt (age 17): *I still haven't heard. Not a single word from anybody. You'd think these colleges would be more prompt in how they handle applications. I mean, it's been two months. I gave them everything they wanted: transcripts, completed applications, referral letters, essays, solid SAT scores, and solid AP test scores—I even did the visitation thing and completed some interviews. Every admissions rep I met with said I was a promising candidate and that they looked forward to receiving my application, but I haven't heard. Not from one. Zip, zero, nada. What if I don't get into any of my top-choice schools? What if I don't get into any colleges at all?*

Darnelle (age 16): *My heart races every time I think about it. I was so scared, man. I'm not afraid to admit it. When my car hit that black ice and catapulted over the embankment, I thought I was a goner, for sure. I mean, my SUV flew over twenty feet. I was airborne! When I saw the boulders on one side and the trees on the other, I thought I was dead. But, miracle of miracles, the truck landed right side up, blew out all four tires on impact, and settled in the grassy dip between the rocks and trees. Not a scratch on me. Wow! What a ride. And I wasn't even speeding. I wonder if this means I'll lose my license.*

Seven teenagers. Seven sets of circumstances. One thing in common. Can you guess what it is?

These fictional blog entries (a blog is an on-line diary open to anyone to read) could have been taken from any of several Internet teen diary Web sites. The circumstances, joys, pressures, and challenges expressed in these entries are typical of those many adolescents face each day. And though the circumstances differ, each includes an element faced by every teenager in North America: stress.

STRESS

We've all experienced it. We can probably describe what it feels like. But, just what is stress? The American Heritage Dictionary defines stress as "an applied force or system of forces that tends to strain or deform a body." In other words, stress could be described as the pressure or demands placed upon us and how we respond to those pressures.

Think of a rubber band. If you hold a rubber band with two hands and pull its ends in opposite directions, you're applying force to the rubber band. You have put the rubber band under stress. The term "stress" here describes both what you are doing with your hands and how the rubber band is affected. The farther and harder you pull, the more stretched-out the rubber band becomes. The more you stretch it, the thinner it gets: The pressure you apply deforms (changes) the shape of the rubber band. If you pull hard enough and far enough, the rubber band will snap.

Or think about play dough. When you roll play dough between your hands, the harder and faster you roll, the more it changes shape. If you move your hands back

> **Stress Defined**
>
> Stress describes both the pressures or demands placed upon us and how we respond to those pressures.

Balancing Act

Stress can cause physical symptoms. A headache is one of the most common.

and forth in a horizontal motion, you form the play dough into a tube or cylinder. If you move your hands in a circular motion, your hand motion shapes the dough into a ball. If you push your hands together keeping the play dough between your palms, the dough squishes flat. The force of your hands presses the play dough into different shapes depending on the strength and type of the force applied, yet in all cases, "stressing the dough" describes both the pressure of your hands on the dough and the impact the pressure has.

When we talk about stress in everyday life, like that described in the teen blogs that opened this chapter, we're really talking about two things: the forces of life (circumstances, events, etc.) that tend to strain us emotionally, mentally, and physically—and how we respond to those forces. Stressors in our lives, whether good or bad, affect us in different ways, just as different pressures on play dough produce different results. All could be said to be "stress." Consider our blogging teens.

> **Samples of "Bad" Stressors**
>
> - family problems
> - sickness
> - conflict
> - peer pressure
> - loneliness
> - too much homework
> - financial problems

> **Samples of "Good" Stressors**
>
> - team tryouts
> - sports competitions
> - auditions or recitals
> - job offers
> - pre-performance jitters
> - preparing for exams

19

Balancing Act

Dirk's parents' divorce announcement made him angry. It made his brother sad.

Becoming a cheerleader gave Missy hope that Joey would notice her, but made her nervous, too.

Mr. Rodriguez's treatment of Angeline made her feel sick and discouraged.

Lauren's busyness forced her into a difficult choice.

Jessie's financial pressures left her exhausted.

Matt's unanswered college applications made him worry about his future.

Darnelle's auto accident scared him so much that his heart still pounded in his chest.

Like hands on play dough, the pressure of each circumstance left its mark on each teen: anger, sadness, nervousness, discouragement, nausea, excitement, hope, confusion, exhaustion, fear, worry, and an adrenaline rush. These teens were stressed!

When we think of stress, we often think negatively: family problems, conflicts with a boyfriend or girlfriend, unfair work expectations, too much homework, an overbearing coach, or an unfair teacher. But stress doesn't have to come from negative events. In fact, stress can occur in pleasant, positive circumstances like getting a job, being asked to a dance, or making the varsity squad. Again, stress describes a force applied, whether good or bad, and the response. Both kinds leave their marks.

Think of the stress a high school baseball player feels when his team is down by one run, it's the bottom of the ninth, bases are loaded, and it's his turn to bat. The situation is actually a positive, hopeful scenario: one RBI will tie the game, two will cinch the win—all he has to do is hit the ball. The batter faces enormous stress that if handled well, will allow him to play his best. Is the situation causing the batter's stress bad? No. Is the player affected? Sure: his palms are no doubt sweaty; his heart is beating

Stress can be caused by many different kinds of situations. For example, choosing a direction in life that is different from the route everyone around you is taking may be admirable and courageous—but it is also a stressful course of action.

hard in his chest; his mind is alert and focused. The "good" stress of being under pressure to play well is impacting his body, much in the same way as the "bad" stress of a near car accident caused Darnelle's heart to race. Both were adrenaline responses, which we will learn about in chapter 3.

Though these two teens faced very different sources of stress (one "good" and one "bad"), the impact on them was similar. Both endured effects of stress.

Stress Is Unavoidable

For North American teens living in the twenty-first century, stress is a way of life. Contemporary times and present-day societies are filled with stress. We live in an age of global warming, environmental concerns, terrorism, threat of nuclear war, relatively new diseases like AIDS and **SARS**, and rapidly changing technology. Just staying current with state-of-the-art computer programs or digital gadgets can be a huge source of stress all by itself, let alone keeping track of our ever-changing world.

Cultural norms and values have changed, too, and teens are caught in the crossfire of mixed messages. What used to be illegal is acceptable behavior now (gambling, for instance). What was considered "wrong" is now

Life is full of stressful situations!

viewed as "right," and in some cases, expected (for example, working mothers). All these changes can cause stress.

Remember that stress never refers to the circumstance alone. As Dr. Vladimir Bernik states in his work *Stress: The Silent Killer*, "It is important to understand that stress always corresponds to a relation between the environment and the individual." Stress doesn't describe only the environment or circumstance, nor does it describe only the person in that environment or circumstance. Stress refers to an *interaction between both*.

Sometimes this interaction is helpful, and sometimes it causes harm. What makes the difference? How we handle it.

In the following chapters, we'll talk about the sources of stress, the specific effects stress can have on us, and ways of managing stress that can help, or hinder, our responses to our circumstances.

2

The Causes of Stress

Andrew felt the familiar tightness in his chest as he settled into his padded seat. After securing his harness, his white-knuckled grasp was the only symptom of his gathering fear. Though his heart thumped wildly inside his chest, his outer demeanor exuded calm confidence and control. It wasn't until his roller coaster car crested the first ascent and plunged nearly two hundred feet into darkness that he lost control and screamed.

Torrey knew he had to do well in this tryout or he'd never make the team. Using every ounce of strength and speed he had, the young track hopeful pushed himself to his limit, setting a new personal best. But would it be good enough?

Angie was tired of hearing her parents fight every night. Instead of soothing melodies, soft music, or the quiet whisper of trees outside, Angie's lullabies were filled with the sounds of bottles breaking, screamed threats, and brutal thumps against the wall. Would it ever end?

"You didn't give me the right change, young man!" The elderly woman in the straw hat and oversized sunglasses snapped at fifteen-year-old Kip. The teenager had only been working at the pool snack stand for a few days, and cashiering was new to him. It was his first real job.

"Er . . . I'm sorry, ma'am, but I thought I counted it out right." Kip tried to explain. "I double checked. Really I did."

"Why, of all the impertinence! Don't you correct me, boy!" The woman wagged her finger in Kip's face. "Didn't anybody ever teach you to mind your elders! Where's your manager? I demand to talk to your boss!"

Amber loved lifeguarding at the Country Club. It was the best job she'd ever had. Until Howard showed up. Sneaky, dirty-old-man Howard. Everybody else thought Howard was a nice retiree who got along great with the younger crowd. Her boss told her to humor him; he said

Stress comes in all shapes and forms. What one person finds stressful may not be for another individual. For instance, many teens enjoy talking on the phone—but other young people may get tense and anxious in the very same situation.

Balancing Act

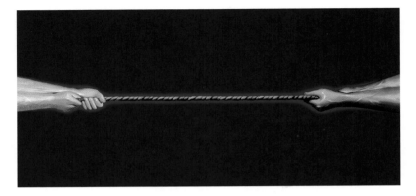

Sometimes stress feels like something being pulled tight inside of you.

Howard was harmless. But Amber's instincts knew differently. She wondered how much longer she'd have to put up with his crass jokes, his suggestive remarks, his pats on her butt, or his leering eyes glued to her chest when she walked by. The guy gave her the creeps. Then she found herself closing up the pool alone one rainy night after ten o'clock. As she turned to lock up the changing rooms, Howard grabbed her by the arm and pulled her behind the door.

Each of these teens faced stress from different sources. In the first two cases (the roller coaster ride and track try-outs), the teens sought out their stress—they chose to experience it. In the last three examples (parents arguing, the *irate* customer, and possible assault), unwanted stress came to these teens from circumstances beyond their control. These scenarios illustrate two facts about stress:

    1. Stress can be something we enjoy and choose (like a roller coaster ride) or it can be

threatening and uninvited (like hearing parents fight or being falsely accused).

2. Stress can be short-term and intense (like the roller coaster ride or the argument with the customer), or it can be long-term and gradually wear you down (like parents arguing every night for weeks, months, or years). Short-term stress is called **acute** stress. Long-term stress is called **chronic** stress.

Acute versus Chronic Stress

Lots of things in the course of the day can cause *acute* (short-term) stress:

- nearly missing the bus
- not being able to open your locker
- fighting with a friend
- being called upon by a teacher
- forgetting your lunch money
- being summoned to the principal's office
- nearly being in an auto accident on the way home from school
- having your computer crash in the middle of writing your English term paper
- arguing with your parents about watching TV on a school night

These are immediate situations that activate an immediate response. Our bodies respond to these stressors in various ways: feelings of nervousness, frustration, or agitation, sweaty palms, increased heart rate, difficulty

29

breathing, feelings of extra energy, clearer thinking, intense emotion, and after all this, a sudden sense of exhaustion. In acute stress, we rev up, then we crash.

Chronic stress takes longer to develop and can take less obvious forms:

- repeated struggles with school work
- ongoing illnesses or disabilities
- fear and tension caused by bullying or continual teasing
- loneliness or feelings of isolation
- anxiety caused by taking on too many activities
- expecting too much of yourself
- watching a loved one get sicker with a **progressive** disease

The symptoms of chronic stress can be subtle, but they are also warning signs that should not be ignored: chronic tiredness, sleep disturbances, inability to concentrate, depression, frequent mood swings, irritability, weight gain or weight loss, and other health symptoms that your doctor can't explain otherwise.

In both acute and chronic stress, we're impacted physically, mentally, and emotionally (we'll see how this happens in the next chapter), so it's important to recognize potential sources of stress in our lives.

Common Sources of Stress

It seems that the causes of stress are as plentiful as the number of researchers who study stress! One researcher,

The Causes of Stress

Dr. George Engel (1913–1999), formerly of the University of Rochester, identified eight primary sources of stress:

- death of a loved one
- acute grief
- threat of loss
- mourning
- loss of status or self-esteem
- personal danger
- the time immediately following danger
- reunion, triumph, or happy ending.

Two other researchers, Dr. Thomas Holmes and Dr. Richard Rahe, developed a list of forty-three specific

> ### Common Causes of Stress for Teens
>
> The University of Minnesota Extension Service, reporting on a survey done in Minnesota on adolescent stress and depression, listed these as the top eight most common life-event stressors in teens:
>
> 1. break up with a boyfriend or girlfriend.
> 2. increased arguments with parents.
> 3. trouble with a brother or sister.
> 4. increased conflict between parents.
> 5. change in parents' financial status.
> 6. serious illness or injury of family member.
> 7. trouble with classmates.
> 8. trouble with parents.

major life events that cause stress and assigned point values to each. This self-test, called "The Life Event Scale," is commonly used today to assess how much stress a person is under. Larger issues are assigned higher point values (for example, death of a spouse counts for 100 points; personal injury or illness counts for fifty-three points; pregnancy counts for forty points; death of a close friend is thirty-seven points, and so on). In general, the higher the total score, the higher the potential for unhealthy stress responses. A total score of over 300 points is considered "severe stress potential."

Still other stress researchers group stress sources other ways: family stress, school stress, relational stress, and so on. For the purposes of this book, we'll divide sources of stress into four categories:

1. stress from health issues or physical conditions
2. stress from outside circumstances beyond our control
3. stress from outside circumstances we can control
4. stress from internal feelings or expectations

Stress from Health Issues or Physical Conditions

Imagine what it would be like to live every day in chronic pain, or with breathing difficulties, or with a fatal disease. Think about how you might feel if you were unable to walk or talk like everyone else. Consider how much time would be involved bathing and getting dressed in the morning if you only had one arm and hand. Picture how frustrating school would be if you couldn't read. Imagine what it would be like if you couldn't do all the things other teens take for granted.

Maybe you don't have to imagine at all. Maybe you live with one of these sources of stress every day.

Learning disabilities, physical challenges, chronic health issues, and psychiatric disorders can all cause significant amounts of stress for teenagers who carry these issues. From physical education classes to sports teams to popularity contests to just getting through the day— these normal activities bring more stress to the lives of adolescents with physical issues than most teens unaffected by health issues can imagine.

Dan is a teenager with *epilepsy*. What should be a normal, exciting rite of passage—getting his driver's license—has him filled with fear: *What if I have a seizure when I drive?*

Bryan is a high school senior with *cerebral palsy*. Instead of looking forward to his senior prom as most teens his age would, he dreads the dance. It's become a symbol of his loneliness and isolation: *What girl would ever want to go with me?*

Thirteen-year-old Katie has a bladder disease that causes her to have difficulty holding her urine. What should be an exciting celebration—four days away at sleepover camp for "outdoor school" with the entire sixth-grade class—has become a source of embarrassment and shame: *If I go, my friends will find out I still wet my bed at night and have to wear diapers.*

These teens can't change their conditions, nor can they help being the way they are. Their physical challenges force them to think about things that most teens never consider. Teens with health issues are forced to face enormous challenges each day that most teens can only imagine. Their health issues add significant stress to their lives.

STRESS FROM OUTSIDE CIRCUMSTANCES BEYOND OUR CONTROL

Michelle's family can't afford to send her to college. If she wants to go, she has to earn a full scholarship or find a way to pay for her schooling on her own.

We use many metaphors for describing the way stress feels. Sometimes people speak of "carrying a heavy load."

34

Items from
"The Life Event Scale Adapted for Teens"

Mary Susan Miller, in her book *Child-Stress: Understanding & Answering Stress Signals of Infants, Children, & Teenagers,* adapted the forty-three items on Holmes' and Rahe's Life Event Scale to better fit stressors faced by children and teens. Here are just a few of her listings:

• death of a parent: 100 points
• divorce of parents: 73 points
• separation of parents: 65 points
• death of a close family member: 63 points
• personal injury or illness: 53 points
• suspension from school: 47 points
• long vacation: 45 points
• anxiety over sex: 39 points
• a good friend moving away: 37 points
• quarreling with parents: 35 points
• family moving or changing schools: 20 points

Again, just 300 points total indicates severe stress potential.

Fourteen-year-old George's father needs a job. The only good offer his dad received is from a corporation in another state. His father decides to take the offered position. It looks like the family, including George, will be moving a thousand miles away.

Balancing Act

When many stressors occur at the same time—like a squadron of fighter planes all taking off at once—we may feel as though life is out of control.

Thirteen-year-old Vanessa's father is an alcoholic. Her mother, who is never home, works long hours to keep the family's finances afloat. Vanessa never knows if her dad will show up to pick her up after basketball practice, or if she'll have to walk to the local bar to find him. Her job is to look out for her younger siblings and try to manage the cooking and laundry, on top of her schoolwork, interests, and running interference between her parents. Vanessa is worn out.

Michelle, George, and Vanessa each experience stress from factors beyond their control. Michelle can't change her parent's income; George can't give his father a job; and Vanessa can't make her father stop drinking. These are all outside circumstances about which these teens can do very little and from which comes great stress.

What other outside circumstances beyond our control can cause stress?

- accidents or unintentional injuries
- the weather
- traffic jams
- death
- divorce
- substance abuse by a loved one
- changes in school policies
- a teacher's grading practices
- school class schedules
- an employer's practices or policies
- other people's actions
- other people's opinions of us
- other people's responses to us
- other people's feelings

Balancing Act

One of the most difficult realities of growing up is realizing that there are some things we just can't control. One of the most difficult of these is accepting that we cannot control or change other people. Sometimes we worsen the stress we experience from situations (or people) we can't control because we haven't accepted our inability to control or change the situation. Appropriate acceptance of our limitations and situations can help reduce our stress.

Stress from Outside Circumstances We Can Control

Francine has three major papers due on Friday. She also agreed to cover for a friend at work after school Wednesday and Thursday nights. She volunteered to tutor other students during her study halls that week, and will be away skiing for the preceding weekend. Francine is completely stressed out about how she's going to get her papers done.

Scott is in a quandary. His travel soccer team is shorthanded for an important game Saturday morning, but his baseball team made the play-offs and they need him to pitch that day. He can't be in two places at once. Scott has a knot in his stomach just thinking about what he must do.

Angie's best friend, Lisa, smokes pot and takes **Ecstasy**. Angie doesn't want to do drugs, but her whole group of friends is moving in that direction. Lisa's single-parent dad will be away for the weekend on business, so she'll have the place to herself. She invites a bunch of friends, including Angie, over to crash at her place for the weekend. Angie knows drugs and alcohol will be involved and that her friends will pressure her to party, but she doesn't want to hurt her friends by refusing to go.

Unlike the previous three teens, these three teens are facing stress from situations over which they do have some control. Francine's stress about homework resulted largely from her busy schedule, her choice to go skiing, her choice to give up her study halls, and her choice to work extra hours during a heavy-homework week.

Scott's stress ultimately came from his choice to participate at a high level in two simultaneous sports. He didn't *have* to join both teams; he *wanted* to.

Angela's stress comes from choosing to remain with a group of friends who won't accept her choice to stay clean and sober. She could make new friends who would support her drug-free decision, but she chooses not to.

Some stress can be of our own making. It can come as a result of choices we make:

- If I choose not to study, I may do poorly in school.
- If I choose to stay up late, I may be exhausted.
- If I choose to have a pet, I may resent the time it takes to care for the animal.
- If I choose to have sex, I may get pregnant or contract a disease.
- If I choose to shoplift, I might get arrested.
- If I choose to drive drunk, I may kill someone with my car.

Balancing Act

All of these things—doing poorly in school, being chronically exhausted, resenting pet care, getting pregnant, contracting an **STD**, getting arrested, or killing someone by driving drunk are huge stressors than can be prevented. We just need to make different choices. You might be surprised how many sources of stress are under your control. Some, like these, are external; they have to do with what's happening around us. Others we find in ourselves.

Stress from Internal Feelings or Expectations

Rhonda was angry with herself after the exam. *How could you be so stupid! You should have studied more. Why didn't you take more time to study the vocab words? You knew they'd be on the test!*

T.J. couldn't help feeling disappointed, and a bit panicked, when he found out that he'd dropped from number two in his class ranking to number seven, out of 523 students in the junior class. He expected more of himself. His goal was to be senior valedictorian, number one in his class. He'd have to work harder, even though he was already investing six hours per night in homework.

I should be able to handle all this, Jolene thought to herself through her tears. *What's wrong with me? I mean, I only do school, work, and one sport each season. It's not that much, really. I don't even have time for friends. Why am I so stressed out?*

Though their ways of showing it differed, Rhonda, T.J., and Jolene fell prey to the very same source of stress: expectations. Rhonda's expectation that she should know everything on the test (a common source of stress in teens) caused her to berate herself. T.J.'s expectation that he should be able to be number one in a class of over five hundred drove him to place impossible demands on himself. Jolene's expectation that she should be able to live without friends left her emotionally unable to cope with her other stressors.

These teens' stress didn't come from other people or circumstances; their stress came from how they saw themselves and what they expected.

We live in a stress-filled world, and stress, it seems, can come from just about anywhere: our bodies, our circumstances, our choices, our thoughts and emotions.

Facing so much stress is sure to have an effect on us— but how? The next three chapters will help us understand how stress affects our bodies, minds, emotions, relationships, and responsibilities.

3

How Stress Affects Your Body, Mind, and Emotions

Have you ever felt an exhilarating rush after surviving a terrifying amusement park ride? That's stress.

Have you ever felt sweaty and nervous when talking to someone to whom you

Balancing Act

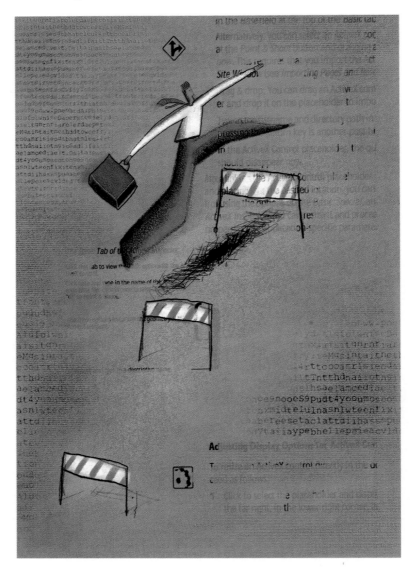

When we're stressed, life may seem like a series of hurdles we have to leap in order to move forward.

44

are attracted? That's stress, too.

Have you ever experienced a rush of speed or strength while running when being chased by an unfamiliar dog? That's stress, as well.

Have you ever gotten nauseated (literally) at the thought of giving a speech in front of your friends? Yep. That, too, is stress.

Stress, if you recall, isn't defined as only the situations that cause stress, but our response to those situations as well. Stress includes how we react mentally, emotionally, and physically to various sources of stress.

Stress is a goofy thing, though. It can produce many different physical symptoms, some pleasant and some intensely unpleasant, yet at its source remains essentially the same biological process. This process is a good thing, at first.

The Body's Self-Protection

Stress (the bodily response) begins as a self-protective mechanism. When you feel threatened, your body reacts by producing extra energy you need to meet the threat. Part of this extra energy production happens when your body's **central nervous system** releases certain chemicals into your brain, causing your body to react in various ways.

Sandy had to work late and found herself walking home alone in the dark. She knew the dangers of being a young girl out alone at night on a deserted street, but she didn't want to call her parents for a ride, and she thought she'd be safe walking the short distance between her job at the

45

corner market and her family's apartment a half-a-block away.

About twenty yards beyond the gated entrance of the shop she just closed, Sandy heard footsteps closing in behind her. Her heart began to race. Her palms grew wet with sweat. She could hear her blood rushing in her ears, yet all the sounds of the city street also echoed with a clarity she hadn't noticed moments earlier. Her vision was sharper than it usually was at night, and she felt especially alert. No more post-work sleepiness for Sandy. Not on this night.

Then she felt someone grab her arm.

Physical Responses to Acute Stress

You breathe faster and harder.
Your heart beats faster.
Your muscles tense up.
Your senses get keener.
You feel more alert.
You feel stronger and more energetic.
You sweat more.
Your mouth gets dry.
Your digestion slows down.

"Sandy" her older brother exclaimed as he swung his sister around to see his face. "I'm glad I found you! What are you doing walking home alone at this time of night? You could get mugged, or worse."

"Oh, Bro," she sighed with relief, "I'm so glad it's you. I was really scared! Will you walk me home?"

How Stress Affects Your Body, Mind, and Emotions

With those words, Sandy could feel the tension ooze from her body. Her breathing slowed again and the sound of the blood rushing through her ears was gone.

Sandy's body had been reacting to her sense of alarm. When she heard footsteps behind her, it's as if her brain silently screamed, *Danger! Possible threat approaching!* and every other organ and system that made up her physique took notice and began to respond. Sandy's body was only doing what it was supposed to do.

Once your body perceives a danger, it releases chemicals that make you more alert and ready for action, just as Sandy experienced. These chemicals cause your heart to beat faster, your rate of breathing to increase, your pupils to get bigger, your blood pressure to rise, your sweat glands to produce more sweat, your sense organs (sight, smell, etc.) to sharpen, and your mouth to dry out. All of a sudden you seem to be able to hear and see better than you could before. You feel energized and alert.

Two specific chemicals released when the body perceives a threat are **hormones** called epinephrine and norepinephrine. These hormones, combined with two chemicals released by the adrenal gland called adrenaline and noradrenaline cause what we call "an adrenaline rush" (those feelings of being energetic, excited, and anxious all at the same time). In one study reported in the Time-Life book entitled *Stress*, researchers linked epinephrine with feelings of fear and norepinephrine with feelings of anger or rage.

These hormones and chemicals cause the body to do amazing things: like other chemicals in the body, they increase blood pressure and heart rate. They also signal the spleen to release more oxygen-carrying red blood cells, the bone marrow to produce more infection-fighting white blood cells, and the blood to clot more quickly (in

47

case of a bleeding wound). These responses prepare the body to deal with and recover from a physical attack, and they continue until your body perceives that the danger has passed.

Your body can also suppress (cut back on) the production of other chemicals to help increase your protective responses. Serotonin, a chemical produced in the brain that helps us fall asleep and stay asleep, is one of the first chemicals the body suppresses during a perceived threat. That is, in part, why we feel so alert.

All of this is well and good for a short-term stressor, like being frightened by footsteps behind you when walking home alone in the dark, or when experiencing a near collision with an automobile. After these short-term crises, your brain signals the rest of the body to relax. When Sandy realized it was her brother's footsteps she heard, the danger had passed, and it was as if her brain said to the rest of the body, *Step down, now. The threat is gone.* With that communication, all Sandy's systems returned to normal.

Self-Protection Gone Haywire

What happens if our brains never give *"The threat is gone"* instruction? That's what happens with chronic stress. When the stressors we face are ongoing, our brains never tell our bodies to relax. Constant stress signals our bodies to keep producing excess chemicals, or to suppress production of other needed substances, which in turn, signal the body to stay in "danger" mode for long periods of time. Our bodies, however, aren't de-

How Stress Affects Your Body, Mind, and Emotions

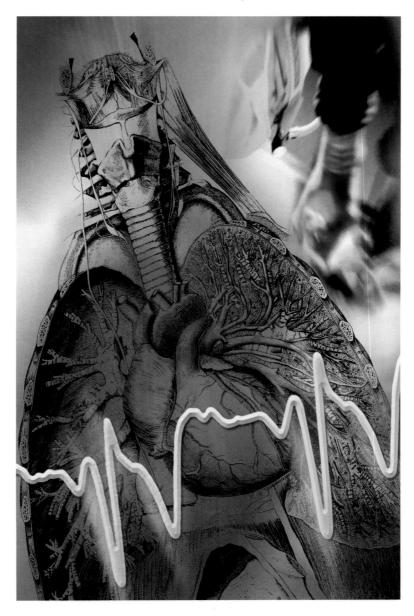

Stress signals our hearts to beat faster and our lungs to work harder.

signed to run this way, and these long-term stress responses can result in or aggravate disease.

Consider how short-term (acute) stress impacts us. Because our normal stress responses affect blood flow, production of blood cells, and heart rate, it's not difficult to imagine how long-term stress can result in cardiovascular disease (diseases of the heart and heart vessels). Because our normal stress responses also impact the production of white blood cells (our bodies' disease-fighting cells), we can see how chronic stress might weaken our immune systems and make us more susceptible to disease and infection. Because these normal re-

Too much stress can increase stomach acid, making a person prone to stomach pain and ulcers.

Diseases or Conditions Made Worse
by Chronic Stress

- high blood pressure
- arrhythmia (irregular heartbeat)
- coronary artery disease
- susceptibility to heart attack and stroke
- rheumatoid and juvenile arthritis
- reflux disease
- peptic ulcers
- irritable bowel syndrome
- Crohn's disease
- asthma
- painful and irregular menstrual periods
- autoimmune diseases
- psychological disorders (including depression)
- most chronic degenerative diseases (muscular dystrophy, cystic fibrosis, etc.)
- migraine and tension headaches

sponses impact chemical substances in the brain, we can understand how chronic stress might result in brain-related disorders, like depression, anxiety disorders, and memory loss. Too much stress takes its toll on our bodies, all because our systems can't get a break.

One symptom of being under too much stress is an inability to sleep. This comes from the body's suppression of the brain chemical serotonin, which we said earlier helps us to sleep well. Without getting an *"it's safe now"* signal, the brain won't produce the serotonin our bodies need and we won't be able to sleep. If danger is real, the brain doesn't want us to sleep.

Balancing Act

When our bodies run perpetually on "danger" mode, something eventually breaks down. The ability to sleep is often the first thing to go.

Real or Imagined: It Makes Little Difference

Interestingly enough, these effects occur whether the threat is real or imagined. The key is what our bodies ***perceive***. If we perceive something as being potentially harmful, whether our perception is accurate or not, our bodies will respond automatically as if the threat was real.

A young child's panic over the boogie monster under his bed is no less a survival response than Sandy's reaction to footsteps closing in. The child's body and Sandy's body respond much the same way (increased heart rate, rapid breathing, etc.), though the child's stress is based on imagination and Sandy's threat definately seemed more real. Both bodies perceive the source of stress as legitimate threats. In both cases they are wrong. The child's monster is imaginary. Sandy's perceived attacker was only her brother who sought to walk her safely home.

Common Symptoms of Too Much Stress

- inability to sleep
- lack of energy
- muscle aches and pains
- anxiety
- irritability
- depression
- headaches

How Stress Affects Your Body, Mind, and Emotions

Fear, uncertainty, doubts, imaginings, negative thoughts—all these can produce a stress response in the body, every bit as much as real, physical, external triggers (like footsteps) can. Even dreams can trigger this protective response. How did your body react to your last nightmare? Did your heart race? Did you feel tense? Did you sweat more? Your body responded even though your mind imagined it all.

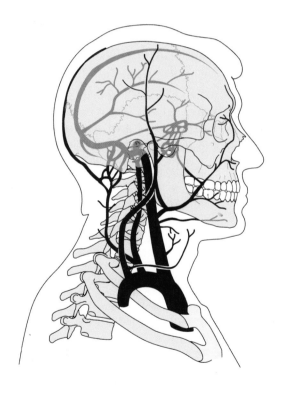

Stress affects circulation and muscle tension. Both factors can contribute to head pain.

Balancing Act

The same thing can happen when we think about a stressful event before it happens or when we relive it after the fact. Anticipating a roller coaster ride (thinking about it ahead of time) creates sheer terror in some people, before they set foot on the ride. Our imagination (thinking about what the ride will be like) can trigger our bodies' stress responses even more than the ride itself.

Worry can have the same effect. Fretting about a test can cause our blood pressures to rise, and give us knots in our stomachs, but then we can be fine for the test itself. Amazing, isn't it, how our minds can trigger physical responses just as powerfully as circumstances can!

Our minds and our bodies work together to keep us healthy and safe, yet they impact each other in mysterious ways that scientists are only just beginning to understand. Stress, we know at the very least, impacts them both. We've seen what stress can do to the body, both through real or imagined stressors. Now let's look at what stress can do to our minds and emotions.

Stress, Mind, and Emotions

The U.S. Centers for Disease Control (CDC) lists suicide as the eleventh leading cause of death for all Americans, and the third leading cause of death for young people between the ages of fifteen and twenty-four. According to Canada's Centre for Suicide Prevention, suicide rates are slightly higher in Canada than in the United States. Combining suicide counts of both countries, it's estimated that more than 33,500 people in Canada and the United States end their lives by suicide each year.

Stress has long been considered a risk factor for suicide—something that makes it more likely for someone to consider killing himself. Why? Because stress can have a significant influence on how we think and feel.

Stress and the Brain

We saw earlier in this chapter that the "danger" signals of acute stress triggered excess production of certain chemicals in the brain and decreased production of others. Some of these chemicals are responsible for activating certain feelings or emotions. Most of these "feeling chemicals" are called neurotransmitters, because they are responsible for carrying (transmitting) messages between nerve cells (neurons) in the brain.

The brain is a complex organ made up of an estimated one hundred *billion* neurons. Each neuron sends and receives electrical messages to and from other neurons. The difficulty is that there is a microscopic space between each nerve cell. Electrical messages can't just jump from one cell to another; they have to be carried by special messengers, the neurotransmitters.

The brain's messaging process is somewhat like the process of calling a friend on the telephone (land line, not wireless). Let's say you have a message you'd like to communicate to your friend. In the brain, that would make you the sending cell called the presynaptic (before the space) neuron. You "fire" a signal to your friend over the space between you (called the synapse) by using the telephone line (the neurotransmitter). Your friend is a receiving cell, called the postsynaptic (after the space) neuron. When you call your friend on the telephone, he has to answer (or pick up) the telephone in order for the message to be received. Communication in the brain works the same way: in order for communication to occur between neurons, the messages must not only be sent, but received.

When we have too many chemical neurotransmitters, messages can flood certain parts of the brain without sufficient receiving cells to pick up the messages. When we have too little of these chemicals, there aren't enough messengers to carry the messages, and communication doesn't occur between cells the way it should.

This disruption in communication between nerve cells in the brain can greatly impact our thoughts and emotions. Not enough of one neurotransmitter—serotonin, for example—can cause us to feel *lethargic*, think dark thoughts, obsess about petty things, lose any sense

---

Stress-Related Feelings in Teens

Though all teens feel these emotions at one time or another, experiencing them frequently or over long periods of time may indicate you're under too much stress:

- apathy (not caring about anything)
- discouragement
- sadness
- weariness
- isolation
- rage
- anger
- fear
- anxiety
- agitation
- the need to withdraw

---

of joy or pleasure, and feel overwhelmed. What does that sound like to you? You probably guessed it: depression.

Depression is only one illustration of how stress can impact our thoughts, emotions, and how our minds work. What other impacts can stress have?

STRESS AND EMOTIONS

Georgia is caught stealing a blouse at a department store.

Justine's best friend accuses her of spreading rumors. Justine knows the accusation is untrue.

A drunk driver kills Bobby's ten-year-old cousin who was walking on a sidewalk minding his own business when he died.

Suzanne worries that she might not take first place in debate competition because of her one major goof.

Todd practiced his violin until his fingers hurt, but he still didn't make it into District orchestra.

Each of these teens faces a kind of threat, danger, or potential harm. They all are experiencing stress. How might they respond emotionally to their situations? How do you think they might feel?

Fear, anger, aggression, shame, resentment, rage, sadness, excitement, nervousness, discouragement—these are all stress-related emotions. Stress not only results in our feeling these emotions, it can also hurt our ability to handle them. Stress may make us feel defensive, grumpy, overanxious, or jumpy. We might overreact, blow up, or cry. We may want to give up in despair.

Some of the physical effects of stress (like fatigue) can make it more difficult for us to process and manage our feelings. How easy is it, for instance, to be patient or to

57

Balancing Act

Ambition—a self-imposed stressor—can have both positive and negative effects. When we are driven by our need to "get ahead," our stress levels may be overwhelming.

think positively when you're absolutely exhausted? Is it any easier when you're well rested (or under less stress)? What a difference a little sleep and reduced stress can make—not just in our emotions, but in our minds.

Stress and the Mind

Johnny walked into his bedroom to get something, but for the life of him, couldn't remember what he was looking for.

Jessica sat down to take her geometry final, an exam for which she had studied, but when she started working on the problems, she couldn't remember basic formulas.

Roya stood behind the podium ready to present her "why you should make me your class president" speech. But as she began speaking, her words didn't come out straight.

Valerie's teacher called on her in class, asking her to name the agricultural crop for which George Washington Carver was most famous. The pre-teen student, a shy and nervous girl with learning challenges, knew the answer to her teacher's question. Peanuts, of course! But that's not what came out of her mouth. What the class heard her say, to their delight, Valerie's embarrassment, and her teacher's horror, was the P-word for a certain part of a boy's anatomy.

What happened to these teens?

Stress. Nothing more. Nothing less.

Stress not only influences our feelings; it influences how well we think and learn. Short-term memory problems, muddled thinking, difficulty recalling things

59

learned long ago, garbling our words, or saying the wrong words can all be symptomatic of stress. Our brains are on overload, if you will. We can only consciously process so much information and stimuli at one time. Chronic stress, because of its physical impact on the brain, prevents us from thinking as clearly as we otherwise would.

This Is Your Body Talking!

So why should we care if stress makes us think or feel like we do? Is it really that important? Yes. It is. Our bodies can't talk to us with words, but they can talk to us with symptoms. Stress can be so subtle that we don't even know we're under too much stress. That's when our bodies start saying, "Enough, already." The effects of stress we've discussed in this chapter are warning signs, or hints that your body can't take much more. According to mental health professionals at the Stress Management Institute the following should be wake-up calls that we're under too much stress. Do you . . .

- have nervous tics or muscle spasms?
- have twitching eyelids?
- pick at your fingers or rub your hands against your body a lot?
- clear your throat or sneeze often?
- catch colds, sniffles, and a runny nose frequently?
- get short of breath or breathe shallowly?
- develop a dry mouth in anticipation of events?
- have pain in your lower back, chest, shoul-

ders, or in the joints?
- experience abdominal pains?
- get indigestion or upset stomach frequently?
- scratch your skin?
- slump when you sit or stand?
- drag your feet when you walk?
- clutch the steering wheel (if you drive)?
- become edgy while standing in line?
- startle easily in response to noises or sudden motion?
- get tension headaches?
- grind your teeth?

If you find that you answer several of these questions "yes," your body is telling you to reduce your stress! These alone may not be your only indicators of being over-stressed. Stress's impact on your relationships and responsibilities can send up red flags, too.

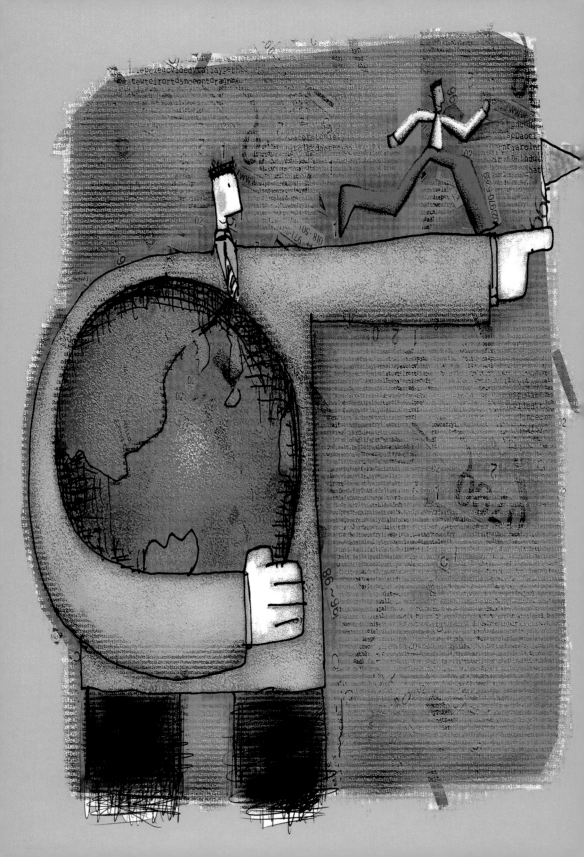

4

How Stress Affects Your Relationships and Responsibilities

Scene One

"Will you just go away and leave me alone?!" Rachel huffed when her concerned mother peeked in the door and asked the moody teen if she was all right.

Balancing Act

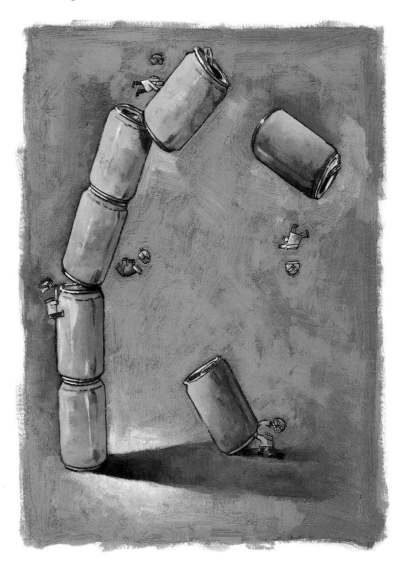

When life seems to come crashing down around us, we may withdraw from others—or we may become angry and resentful.

"I was just concerned, Rach," her mom offered. "You've seemed a bit edgy lately."

"Just back off, Mom. I'm fine. I just want to be left alone. There's nothing you can do about it anyway." With that the teen slumped on her bed and looked away.

"About what, sweetie?"

"Nothing. Nothing at all. Just go away."

Fifteen-year-old Rachel normally confided in her mother. The two shared a special relationship being the only two females in a house full of males. It was unlike Rachel to retreat and withdraw, but that's exactly what she did. And her mother didn't know what to do.

Scene Two

"And now Jody will read the minutes from the last meeting. Jody?"

All eyes of the student council fell on Jody McBain, Student Council Secretary. Her face flushed when she realized they were all waiting for her to speak.

"Ah . . . well . . . er . . . I forgot to bring the minutes with me to school today. They're home in my minutes folder."

"You didn't bring them?" Ann, the Student Council President asked incredulously.

"I meant to, really, I did. I just forgot." Jody fidgeted in her seat.

"But you have all the information about our class trip in that folder!" Ann harped. "How are we going to plan anything now? This meeting is a waste of time if we don't have that information. Can you drive home and get them, like now?"

"I guess so," Jody conceded. "Can you wait? I can be back in twenty minutes."

"We'll adjourn for a twenty minute recess then," the president clucked, smacking the desk with her gavel.

65

"But be quick!" she called after her retreating secretary.

Jody was mortified that she'd forgotten something so basic. What was happening to her?

Scene Three

Barry vegged in front of the TV set. He hadn't moved from his spot on the couch since he arrived home from school.

"Barry, don't you have homework to do?" his father called out to him from the kitchen. It was approaching dinnertime and Barry still hadn't cracked a book.

"Yeah, I suppose," he replied. "There's nothing any good on anyway," he mumbled to himself.

The lanky teenager ambled out of the family room, through the kitchen, into the hall, and up the stairs to his room. He was in low gear today, and he couldn't seem to concentrate. Every time he tried to read, he found him-

---

How Stress Ruins Relationships

- Stress makes us grumpy and irritable to be around.
- Stress reduces our ability to be patient.
- Stress makes us forgetful.
- Stress makes it easy for us to overreact.
- Stress makes us more self-focused.
- Stress distracts us, making it difficult to pay attention to someone else.
- Stress can make us want to hide or withdraw from our friends.

How Stress Affects Your Relationships and Responsibilities

Too much stress can make us "burn out," so that we are emotionally unable to participate in the normal give-and-take of relationships.

self dozing off. When he tried to think, he daydreamed while staring out the window. He finally gave up.

Turning on his computer, he settled in for another long evening of gaming. It was a pleasant escape.

Rachel, Jody, and Barry are all under stress, just as the other teens mentioned in this book have been. But stress affects each person differently.

Rachel is moody and withdrawn. Her relationship with her mother, once close and comfortable, is now awkward and strained. Neither is quite sure how to handle this change.

Jody, normally an ***overachieving perfectionist***, is starting to allow details to fall through the cracks. She forgot her meeting notes and previous meeting minutes—something she hadn't done in three years of being a class officer. And the first half of the meeting was a waste of time thanks to her oversight. Jody's stress caused her to miss details.

How Stress Hurts School Performance

- Stress distracts us, making it hard to listen or pay attention.
- Stress impairs memory, making it difficult to recall facts.
- Stress makes us sleepy, making it easy to make careless mistakes.
- Stress gives us "brain fog," making it hard to think clearly.
- Stress can make us sick, leading to more missed days of school.

Sometimes two individuals may react to the same stress levels in very different ways. While one person is spurred on to achieve still more, another may be overwhelmed and discouraged.

Barry's made him unable to concentrate at all. He used to be a motivated student. He enjoyed his classes, played sports, and hated TV. In recent weeks, though, TV had become his staple in the evenings. All he seemed to want to do was escape. His studies, and his college prospects, suffered because of his low motivation and inability to concentrate.

Balancing Act

The struggles each of these teens encountered are common results of stress. In the previous chapter, we saw how stress affects the body, mind, and emotions. If stress affects these things, then it will certainly affect how we interact with people and how we perform our tasks as well. Consider our three teens again.

Rachel's blow-out with her mom drove a wedge between the once close pair.

Jody's oversight not only wasted everyone else's time, it caused others to lose faith in her ability to handle her role as secretary.

Barry's lethargy caused his grades to fall and ruined some college prospects.

Relationships and responsibilities. Both can be harmed when we allow ourselves to carry too much stress.

The Ugly Side of Stress

We learned in the previous chapter that stress can cause us to become irritable or grumpy. Just how well do irritable people get along with others?

We learned stress can damage our memories and rob us of the ability to sleep. Just how well in school can someone do who can't remember his math facts or stay awake to read?

We learned that stress ultimately distracts us. Just how closely can someone listen if his mind is wandering light years away?

Understanding the effects of stress on our minds and emotions allows us to realize just how damaging stress

How Stress Affects Your Relationships and Responsibilities

Too much stress can make a person "explode" into verbal or physical violence.

can be to our relationships with friends, family, and co-workers, and to our abilities to perform at work or school.

As serious and hurtful as these effects might be, stress can have even scarier consequences.

When Stress Results in Violence

Most Americans are familiar with the tragic events that occurred on April 20, 1999, when two seniors at

---

Sad Stats

According to the National Youth Violence Prevention Resource Center, nearly 30 percent of youth in the United States (or over 5.7 million) are estimated to be involved in bullying as either a bully, a target of bullying, or both. That's enough kids (assuming two children per incident) to be involved in over 7,800 incidents of bullying every day for an entire year, or 325 incidents every hour, or just over five bullying incidents every minute.

Columbine High School, fed up with being teased, killed a dozen students and a teacher and wounded more than twenty others. But are you familiar with these other incidents (condensed from the Infoplease Crime Data resource site):

March 5, 2001 in California: A fifteen-year-old killed two people and wounded thirteen others by firing from a bathroom at a high school.

March 7, 2001 in Pennsylvania: A teenager shot and wounded another student in the school cafeteria. The fourteen-year-old was depressed and frequently teased.

November 12, 2001 in Michigan: A seventeen-year-old took two hostages at a learning center before killing himself.

January 15, 2002, in New York: A teenage shooter wounded two students at a high school.

How Stress Affects Your Relationships and Responsibilities

April 14, 2003 in Louisiana: Four teenagers killed one fifteen-year-old and wounded three others at a high school.

April 24, 2003 in Pennsylvania: A fourteen-year-old killed the school principal before killing himself.

September 24, 2003 in Minnesota: A fifteen-year-old killed one student and wounded another at a high school.

> ### Thinking About Suicide? Call This Number!
>
> If you or someone you know is thinking about suicide, call:
>
> 1-800-SUICIDE (1-800-784-2433)
> or visit www.hopeline.com. on the Internet

All these cases involved student perpetrators of violence. Like overstretched rubber bands, these kids snapped, and people lost their lives. Stress can, indeed, produce scary results.

The National Survey of American Attitudes on Substance Abuse (an annual back-to-school survey conducted by Columbia University's National Center on Addiction and Substance Abuse) found that highly stressed teens are twice as likely as teens with less stress to smoke, drink, get drunk, and use illegal drugs.

Balancing Act

The National School Safety and Security Services linked stress, including specific stressors, to a teen's propensity to commit violent acts or kill, which can be seen by the tragedies described on pages 72 and 73. The

When life seems full of jagged points . . . and you feel like a balloon ready to pop . . . it's time to get some help.

How Can I Tell If Someone Is Ready to Snap?

The American Psychological Association lists these warning signs as indicators of potential imminent violence:

- loss of temper on a daily basis
- frequent physical fighting
- significant vandalism or property damage
- increased use of drugs or alcohol
- increased risk-taking behaviors
- detailed plans to commit acts of violence
- announcing threats or plans for hurting others
- enjoying hurting animals
- purchasing or carrying a weapon

If someone you know exhibits any of these behaviors, keep yourself safe, don't spend time alone with this person, and tell a trusted authority (teacher, counselor, religious leader, policeman, etc.).

American Psychological Association estimates that one in twelve high school students is threatened or injured with a weapon each year, and that students between the ages of twelve and twenty-four face the highest risk of becoming the victim of violence. Stress can lead teens to hurt others or commit crimes.

Though the reasons behind specific acts of teen violence can be difficult if not impossible to identify, most experts agree that stressors of various kinds play a contributing role. These stressors can lead to violence among strangers, friends, and loved ones. They can even cause someone to harm himself.

Warning Signs of Suicide

The National Mental Health Association (NMHA) asserts that four out of five teens who attempt suicide give clear prior warnings. The NMHA lists these behaviors as critical warning signs:

- suicide threats, direct and indirect
- obsession with death
- poems, essays, and drawings that talk about or illustrate death
- dramatic changes in personality or appearance
- irrational, bizarre behavior
- overwhelming feelings of guilt, shame, or reflection
- changes in eating or sleeping patterns
- severe drop in school performance
- giving away belongings

If a friend displays these behaviors, take these warnings seriously and get help immediately.

A Bullied Teen

A few years ago, a teenager stayed home from school, called his father to say "goodbye," then held a .22 revolver against his head and pulled the trigger. He completed his suicide just six short days after his thirteenth birthday. Why? A fatal combination of bullying and the depression he experienced as a result of that stress. Just four months earlier, the then-twelve-year-old sixth-grader had been severely beaten by a bully at school, who later threatened to kill the terrified teen.

The National Institute of Mental Health estimates that in 1996, more teenagers and young adults died of suicide than from cancer, heart disease, AIDS, birth defects, stroke, pneumonia, influenza, and chronic lung disease combined. Suicide was the second-leading cause of death among college students that year, the third-leading cause of death among fifteen-to-twenty-four-year-olds, and the fourth-leading cause of death among ten-to-fourteen-year-olds. There's no doubt about it: stress can kill.

The sad fact is that many of these deaths could have been prevented. According to the National Alliance for the Mentally Ill, the feelings that lead to teen suicide are highly treatable. If the sources of these feelings, including the stressors that cause them, can be addressed, lives can be saved. But how do we address them?

The most effective way of dealing with the stressors in our lives is to avoid unhealthy coping mechanisms, which will be covered in the next chapter, and to embrace those strategies that bring healthy change, found in the last chapter of this book.

5

HANDLING STRESS, PART ONE:

Flight Isn't Always Bad

Bullying Brutus cornered Cowering Chris in the boy's restroom, grabbed the frightened pre-teen by the shirt collar and demanded, "Gimme your lunch money, worm!"

Balancing Act

Cowering Chris, paralyzed with fear, closed his eyes and frantically whispered to himself, *This isn't really happening. No. It's not real. If I ignore him long enough he'll just go away. Please go way, please go away, please go away. . . .*

"What wrong wich you, worm, cancha hear me? I said gimme your lunch money!"

Chris didn't reply. His arms hung limp at his sides while he kept his eyes closed and wished for his tormentor to disappear.

"Last chance before I rearrange your face, punk. Fork it over!" the bully persisted, tightening his grasp on his frightened classmate's shirt.

The squeak of the bathroom door as someone else entered made Bullying Brutus relax his grip, and in a split second, Cowering Chris was gone.

We all face stress. It's part of life. Sometimes, as we learned earlier in this book, stress is acute and temporary (like almost being in an auto accident); other times it can be chronic (like being in a difficult home environment or having a long-term disease). Sometimes the stress is good stress that helps our bodies do what needs to be done (like the tension we feel before performing on stage or participating in a sport). Other times the stress is bad stress that wears us out and harms our bodies (like the stress that comes from struggling in school year after year). Whatever the source of stress, whatever the type of stress, we will respond, but there are only so many options. American physiologist Walter Bradford Cannon (1871–1945), originally summarized these responses into two broad categories: "fight or flight." After studying bodily changes in people facing certain stressors, he concluded that human beings, when threatened, attacked, or fearing harm, will instinctively respond in one of two ways: either face the stressor head-on (fight it), or run away from the stressor (flee from it). Hence the term, "fight or flight."

This fight or flight response can show up in different behaviors. In this chapter's opening scenario, Cowering Chris chose to flee by pretending his captor wasn't there, wishing that he would go away, and then by physically leaving the bathroom at the first opportunity. His "flight" response didn't start with the creak of the bathroom door as someone else came in; it began the moment Bullying Brutus grabbed his shirt collar. Some of his "flight" response was internal (in his mind), some external (closing his eyes), and some took the form of action (leaving the room). But they were all flight responses. In this chapter, we'll look at several of the forms our responses can take, some healthy and some not-so-healthy, but all of which are common ways of dealing with stress. First, let's look at responses that can be various forms of "flight."

Ways We Attempt to Flee Stress

1. We can pretend the stressor doesn't exist. ("If I ignore it, it will go away.")

When Cowering Chris denied to himself that he was being bullied again, then chose to deal with it by wishing for Bullying Brutus to go away, he was in what psychologists call "denial." He simply didn't believe that Brutus would really beat him up. He handled the stress of being threatened by a bully by denying that the bully would really harm him.

81

Balancing Act

Denial sees nothing, when in fact,
you're surrounded by attacking tigers.

Denial Isn't All Bad

Denial is the voice inside of us that says, "This isn't happening to me." "I don't believe it." "There must be some mistake." Denial is actually a built-in way we protect ourselves from being overwhelmed by bad or scary news, like being told we have cancer or hearing about a good friend's death. It buys us time to process the information bit by bit until we can accept it. Denial becomes harmful, however, when it prevents us from ultimately accepting or facing reality. If we never accept the stressful news, we won't find ways to deal with it.

Denial is a common, even necessary, **coping mechanism**, but it isn't healthy if we stay there. When we deny the reality of certain stressors in our lives, we aren't coping; we're just running from our problems. If we're stressed with too much homework and blow off studying for a quiz because we deny that the teacher will give the quiz, what happens when we show up for class the next day and learn that he is, in fact, giving a quiz? We're in trouble. We'll probably fail the quiz, and instead of reducing our stress, our denial compounded it.

Or what about the student who denies that his parents are divorcing, even though they've stated their intention. to do so and have filed court documents to start the process? The student is only prolonging the issue. His denial won't prevent the divorce from happening (it will anyway), but his denial will make it that much harder to deal with the divorce when it is finalized. Denial doesn't solve anything. It just delays our having to deal with the issues, which become more complicated with each delay.

2. We can pretend the stressor is smaller than it is. ("This is no big deal.")

When seventeen-year-old Hilary learned that she didn't get into the college of her choice, she shrugged it off, saying, "So what. There are plenty of other schools. It's not a big deal." That would have been fine had the high school senior really felt that way, but she didn't. Inside she was deeply disappointed, angry, and heartbroken. Her pretend **nonchalance**, a mechanism **mental health professionals** call "minimization," was the coping mechanism she used to avoid the pain of facing her true feelings.

Minimization, however, can have disastrous effects. By not admitting or dealing with her feelings, Hilary's anger and heartache went unexpressed and brewed inside her until they vented themselves in other ways. The normally pleasant teenager became agitated and irritable with everyone for several days, until one afternoon, about a week after receiving her rejection letter, in an episode of road rage, she accelerated too fast while attempting to pass a slower driver, caught her front bumper on the car ahead, and lost control of her vehicle. The resulting accident, injuries, hospitalization, and **rehab** prevented the teenager from going to any college anywhere until a year later. Even Hilary was shocked when she recalled how angry she'd been when she attempted to pass the other car. Her only explanation was that she was angry about not getting into the school she wanted to attend and that she vented her anger through reckless driving.

The consequences of Hilary's minimization happened fairly soon after she received her college notice. Other

*Minimization sees pussycats
where attacking tigers are ready to pounce.*

people suffer consequences of minimization over much longer periods of time.

Minimization that leads to **suppressed** anger, for example, can cause clinical depression, or any one of the many physical consequences of chronic stress identified in chapter three. Stress not dealt with, either through denial or minimization, will take its toll on us one way or another. We can't pretend it's not there or make it out to be less than it really is without harming ourselves or others.

3. We can try to hide from the stressor (through addictions, avoidance, and procrastination).

We've all known people who, instead of working on an assignment or doing an unpleasant chore, put off dealing with the stressor by watching TV, going to a movie, playing video games, chatting on the phone, cruising the Internet, or heading to the mall. Truth be told, we've done these things ourselves. Have you ever delayed making a big decision because it just seemed too hard to make? Have you ever put off working on a book report until the very last minute because you just didn't want to do it? Have you ever had to cram for finals because you were too busy doing other things to study ahead of time? Maybe you were procrastinating.

Avoidance and procrastination are delay tactics. They are ways of putting off the difficulty of dealing with our sources of stress. Imagine having an argument on the telephone with a good friend. When you saw her in school or at work the next day, wouldn't you be tempted to avoid her? By avoiding her, you put off having to deal with the pain of facing her in person after your blow out.

But avoidance and procrastination don't make stressors disappear. They don't change anything. Like denial, they just delay what has to be faced, making it all the harder to deal with later. By avoiding the good friend with whom you fought (in the previous example), you only it make it possible for her feelings to become bitter and hardened, making reconciliation more difficult as time goes by. By procrastinating on a school project, you end up having the same amount of work to do and even less time in which to do it. By putting off the chore of doing laundry, more dirty clothes have time to pile up, making the chore even bigger than before. The result of all these delays? More pressure. More stress. Avoiding and procrastinating simply don't help. Neither does getting high.

Hiding from the stressor.

Balancing Act

*Exaggeration sees prowling, ferocious tigers
where only pussy cats reside.*

When stress is extreme, we might be tempted to avoid the stressors by using a chemical means of escape: drugs or alcohol. Like avoidance and procrastination, escaping into drugs or alcohol doesn't solve anything; we have to "come down" sometime. Then things are only worse. Not only do we have to deal with the original issue, but we have to face the consequences of our drug use, too.

Avoidance, procrastination, and chemical means of escape may help us hide from our stress, but they don't equip us to deal with it effectively.

4. We can make the stressor bigger than it really is. ("I'll just die if. . ." "Everybody. . ." "No one. . ." "Never. . .")

When stressed out about situations or relationships, instead of denying, avoiding, or minimizing, we sometimes think in extremes: "If I don't do this *no one* will like me." "I'm *never* going to get over this." "She *always* treats me this way." "He'll *never* forgive me." "*All* my teachers *hate* me." "I'll be stuck here *forever.*" We think in black-and-white, all-or-nothing terms. "No one," "never," "always"— these are the terms of exaggeration that can take one event or situation, blow it out of proportion, and make it the rule. The reality is that our extreme statements probably aren't true.

When a car breaks down, for example, and we think, *We'll never get home,* our thought is most likely false. The truth is that we will eventually get home; it just may not be when we planned.

Or let's say something embarrassing happens in school—we forget our lines in a school play, or we lose the student government election to kid we dislike. We might think something like, "I'll never live this down," or "I'll die if I have to go to school," or "Everyone will laugh at me." Chances are, within a week or two, the whole thing will be forgotten. Everyone can't possibly laugh because not everyone even knew about what happened to begin with. And going to school most likely won't result in our literal death. Will facing our friends be uncomfortable? You bet. Painful? Perhaps. But it won't truly last forever, only a few people will notice, and it certainly won't kill us.

We do like exaggerating though. By making the problem bigger than it really is, we give ourselves permission to react in extremes: to panic, to have a tantrum, to lose our tempers, to cry, or to become hysterical—all possible responses to stress. Though these expressions allow us to vent our emotions, often inappropriately, they don't really address the source of our stress, nor do they help us face it. They can often do more harm than good.

5. We can remove ourselves or the stressor. ("I need to get out of here." "I quit." "I give up.")

"Well, if these other strategies don't work," we might ask, "why not just remove the source of stress, or get out of the situation? Then we won't have to face it at all." This may sound extreme, but in some situations, especially when physical health, safety, and survival are involved, removal may be the only healthy alternative.

Take the case of a student living in an abusive home environment. Talk about stress! He comes home every afternoon from school never knowing what he'll find. Will his father be passed out drunk on the sofa, will he just act stupid, or will he become violent again? Will the teenager get pummeled this time, or will it be his mother's turn to stop his father's flailing fists? To stay safe, either the teen and his mom need to get out of the house and situation, or the abuser needs to be removed from the home.

When Is Removal the Best Option?

- If the stressor threatens your health or life (intentional threat).
- If the stressor endangers your health or life (unintentionally).
- If the stressor is illegal or causes you to break the law.
- If the stressor causes you to violate strongly held beliefs or morals.
- If you are truly incapable of handling the stressor, even with help and support.
- If the stressor causes harmful physical symptoms.
- If you've done all you can to responsibly and healthfully handle the stress, yet the stressor worsens or remains unchanged.

The same would be true for a girl who finds herself being abused by a boyfriend. Her safety may depend on getting out of the relationship and away from the person who is abusing her. All the coping strategies in the world may not protect her from being browbeaten, assaulted, raped, or killed by an obsessed lover bent on controlling her. Removal may be the only safe means of dealing with this kind of stress.

When removal doesn't happen in these situations, the results can be tragic, even deadly. The National Child Abuse and Neglect Data System (NCANDS) reported that an estimated 1,300 children died in 2001 because of child abuse or neglect. The U.S. Department of Justice found that nearly half of the 500,000 rapes and sexual assaults reported to the police by women in the United States were committed by friends, partners, or other people the victims knew personally. The U.S. Centers for Disease Control (CDC) reports in another survey done of one thousand female college students, that over half had been sexually assaulted, and 43 percent of these assaults had been committed by "steady dating partners." Violence is an extreme stressor that if not dealt with can have lasting, life-altering effects.

But not every situation calls for, or even allows for, removing the source of stress. Not all situations are that extreme. Take homework—hardly as extreme a stressor as physical violence, but a real source of stress nonetheless. When homework becomes overwhelming, we may be tempted to find a way to remove the stress, but in all like-

---

Samples of Situations Where Removal Might Be the Best Option

- When someone threatens to hurt you.
- When working in a smoke-filled restaurant aggravates your asthma.
- When a group of friends pushes you to commit a crime.
- When a boyfriend pushes you to have sex even though you don't want to.
- When, after being assaulted in school and seeking counseling, you still can't walk down the hallway where the assault occurred without panicking.
- When you develop an ulcer from the pressure of your chemistry class.
- When, despite taking all the right steps, a bully's harassment intensifies.

*Removal physically takes the tigers away
or takes us away from the tigers.*

lihood the teacher won't cancel the assignment, and if we're under the age of sixteen, we can't legally drop out of school. We're stuck. The source of stress can't be removed, nor can we remove ourselves from the stressor. What are we supposed to do then?

93

Tips for Handling Bullies

The way you deal with a bully, of course, depends on what is happening. But in general, these tips should help.

1. Ignore him and walk away. Sometimes this is enough. But sometimes this will make the bully angrier.
2. Use your mouth, not your muscles. In other words, yell, tell him to get away from you, tell him to leave you alone, but DON'T FIGHT him.
3. Try to work out your differences in a safe environment. Ask him why he's picking on you. Try to get him to explain his actions. Try to reason with him.
4. Tell someone. Let your friends know what's going on. Recruit them to go with you so you don't have to walk alone. Use a buddy system.
5. Befriend the bully. This is the last thing he'll expect. Not only will your invitation take him by surprise, but most bullies are lonely and hurting. Your friendship may be what he needs to change.
6. If you feel physically threatened or that you're in danger, tell an adult or call the police. Bullying is a form of assault, and it is against the law.

Or what about students like Cowering Chris? As much as he may have wanted to move to another district or switch classrooms or rearrange his schedule to avoid his tormentor, the reality was Chris was going to have to see Bullying Brutus every day in the halls or in the cafeteria or in class. He couldn't avoid him forever, nor could he pretend he wasn't there. It would only be a matter of time until Brutus attempted to extort lunch money from Chris again. What would he do then? What would you do?

There is another option. Instead of denying, minimizing, avoiding, overreacting, or removing ourselves, we can face the stressor head-on, as we'll see in the last chapter.

6

HANDLING STRESS, PART TWO:

Facing Stress Head-On

Let's revisit the bully scenario from the previous chapter. This time, instead of choosing to flee from his tormentor, Cowering Chris decides to face Bullying Brutus.

"Yo, worm! You got lunch

money for me today?" Bullying Brutus sneered as he cornered Cowering Chris in the locker room.

"Get away from me, Brutus," Chris said more loudly than he needed to as he backed up against the wall. The fact that he even replied took Brutus by surprise.

"What, the worm has a voice?" Brutus didn't seem to know what to do.

"Ye . . . yeah! I do have a voice." Chris said, straightening himself, mustering his courage, and standing just a bit taller than he was before. "And I'll use it. You can't scare me into giving you money anymore."

"Everything all right, Chris?" a third voice called from the other side of the lockers. It was the worm's best friend, Jason.

Brutus glanced over his shoulder, then back at Chris.

"Yeah, everything's cool," Chris called out. "I was just on my way out."

The smaller teen pushed past the bully, who still seemed unsure of what to do. Then Chris turned and said something quietly to Brutus so Jason wouldn't hear. "You know, Brutus, people wouldn't hate you so much if you weren't so mean. Try being nice for a change. Who knows? You might even find some friends who are willing to share their lunches with you instead of you stealing money all the time."

With that, Chris walked around the lockers, joined his friend Jason, and headed out to gym.

In the first bully scenario, Chris fled from his source of stress. In the second, he faced it.

How can we learn to face and manage our stress instead of fleeing from it? Three ways:

- change the stressor,
- change ourselves, or
- learn to live with the stress in healthy ways.

How to Face Stress

1. We can work to change the stressor. ("How can the circumstance change?")

In our bully situation, this would not have worked. There was nothing Chris could do to change Brutus. There are times, however, when our sources of stress can be changed. Let's look at homework, for example.

Fifteen-year-old Christine is overwhelmed because a huge science project is due at the end of the week and she knows she can't possibly finish in time. One possible way for her to handle her stress would be to ask for an extension on the project's due date—she could ask her teacher if she can turn the project in on Monday instead of Friday. If the teacher agrees, even though he charges her ten points per day late, the source of Christine's stress has changed (the due date), and her stress is reduced. With the added time to work on the project over the weekend, Christine feels like she can finish the assignment well and turn it in on Monday. The project still needs to be completed—she hasn't removed the stressor—but it has become more manageable.

What if Christine's teacher says no? Then Christine could change how she planned to do the project, perhaps making it less involved. By changing her approach to the project or how much detail she includes, the project could become more manageable and, again, her stress would be reduced.

Changing the stressor can be an effective way to deal with stress if the stressor is an event, thing, or situation. Sixteen-year-old Jay feels pressured because he's been saving up for a top-of-the-line, brand-name gaming computer, but knows he won't have enough money to

> ### Samples of Stressors I CAN Change
>
> - how many hours I work
> - how many activities I'm involved in
> - how much money I spend
> - which friends I hang out with
> - how much time I spend on a homework
>   project

buy it in time for the next net play he has scheduled with his friends. Jay could choose to go with a cheaper brand, a mid-grade computer that is acceptable, just not top-of-the-line, or a generic processor, all of which would greatly reduce the price of the system and make it affordable for him to buy in time for the net play. Or he could choose to wait and not purchase the new computer just yet. By changing the stressor (the type of computer he was willing to buy, or the date by when he purchased it), Jay could reduce his stress.

While it is possible for us to change things or situations, as Jay and Christine did, we cannot change other people. When the source of our stress is relational (parents, a boyfriend or girlfriend, a boss, a fellow employee, a team member, a coach, a sibling, a friend, etc.) we can't force the stressor (the other person) to change. We can only look within ourselves to see how we may be contributing to the situation.

2. We can work to change ourselves to better handle the stressor. ("How can I change?")

Carmen thought her best friend Tiffany never seemed to listen to her. Whenever they got together it seemed like they always did what Tiffany wanted to do. Though she really liked Tiffany, and they'd been friends since grade school, Carmen was frustrated because she felt used.

What could Carmen do?

Well, Carmen could do many things. She could dump Tiffany (remove the stressor), but she doesn't really want to do that. She could pretend nothing was wrong (deny or minimize), but she'd end up only getting angrier and feeling more used. She could point out all of Tiffany's faults, but Tiffany would only get defensive and it wouldn't make Tiffany change.

Carmen chose to look at herself. She asked herself these kinds of questions:

Does Tiffany know how I feel? Have I ever really told her?

Have I been honest when Tiff suggested things to do? Like, when she suggested going bowling, did I say, "Oh all right," when I didn't really want to go, or did I tell her that I'd rather do something else?

What have I been doing (unconsciously) that could make Tiffany think it's okay to treat me this way?

After looking at their relationship, and her role in the relationship, Carmen discovered that she hadn't really been honest with her friend. They always did what

---

Samples of Stressors I CANNOT Change

- other people
- illnesses
- physical disabilities
- learning disabilities
- death
- accidents or injuries

Balancing Act

When you are stressed, you can choose to release tension in ways that are not harmful to yourself or others.

Tiffany suggested because Carmen never found the courage to object.

After talking with Tiffany, Carmen was shocked and pleasantly surprised to learn that her friend was tired of coming up with activity ideas. She not only welcomed Carmen's suggestions but wanted to do them. What could have been a huge, ongoing strain in their relationship became a source of growth for them both, all because Carmen chose to handle this stressor by examining herself and learning to change.

Other self-changes can be made to handle corresponding stressors. Is insufficient time for homework a major source of stress? Perhaps learning how to better manage time or how to plan long-term projects more effectively will solve the problem. Is being unable to find

---

Ways I Can Change Myself

- I can change my thoughts.
- I can change my attitudes.
- I can change how I express my feelings.
- I can change how I communicate.
- I can change how I respond to other people.
- I can change how I respond to circumstances.

---

things in the morning wreaking havoc on getting out the door on schedule? Creating a checklist or a better organizational plan would help. Is busyness making you feel stressed-out and overwhelmed? Maybe changing your expectations and dropping a few activities would help you feel more rested and less stressed.

Balancing Act

Self-change can be an appropriate, healthy way to manage stress. But sometimes there is nothing we can do to change ourselves or our situations. Sometime stress is just a fact of life we are powerless to change. Then what should we do?

3. When stressors cannot be changed, we can learn healthy ways of living with and managing the stress.

When we can't change the stressor, and can't change ourselves or our circumstance, the next best thing is to do all we can to equip ourselves to handle stress in a healthy way physically, mentally, and emotionally.

PHYSICALLY HANDLING STRESS

We saw in earlier chapters that stress, especially chronic stress, can hurt our bodies and compromise our health. It makes sense, then, that taking steps to improve our physical health would better prepare us for times of stress. Taking just a few simple steps can greatly increase our physical ability to handle stress.

1. Eat well.

That means eat a balanced diet. Don't fill up on junk food, but eat healthy foods that will give your body the energy it needs. The U.S. Department of Agriculture's (USDA) Food and Nutrition Information Center (FNIC) recommends a diet higher in breads, cereals, pasta, fruits, and vegetables, and one low in fats. When you look at the dietary recommendations listed in the USDA's Food Guide Pyramid below, how are you doing?

2. Eat regularly.

It isn't enough to eat the right foods; we need to eat the right foods at the right times. How often do you skip meals? How many times this week did you run out the door without breakfast? The U.S. FNIC recommends eating at least three meals each day and including foods

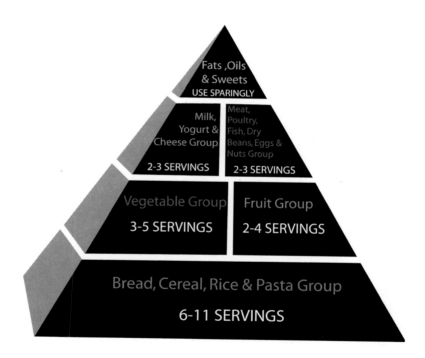

Fats ,Oils & Sweets
USE SPARINGLY

Milk, Yogurt & Cheese Group

Meat, Poultry, Fish, Dry Beans, Eggs & Nuts Group

2-3 SERVINGS

2-3 SERVINGS

Vegetable Group

3-5 SERVINGS

Fruit Group

2-4 SERVINGS

Bread, Cereal, Rice & Pasta Group

6-11 SERVINGS

The Food Pyramid provides a guide for eating a balanced diet.

from the major food groups at each meal. You can also eat four or five smaller meals evenly spaced throughout the day if you'd prefer, and still get the nutrition you need. The FNIC also strongly cautions against skipping breakfast. When we skip breakfast, our bodies don't get the nutrition they need to function at their best. Our ***metabolisms*** slow down and our blood sugars can drop, making us sleepy and irritable. Skipping breakfast only lowers our threshold for handling stress.

A Nation of Skippers

A report published by the Ohio State University Extension's Family and Consumer Science Department found that as many as 48 percent of girls (nearly one out of two) and 32 percent of boys (one out of three) do not eat breakfast every day.

---

3. Get enough sleep.

It's an established fact that most teenagers are sleep deprived. According to a National Sleep Foundation study, 60 percent (or three out of five) of people under the age of eighteen complain of daytime sleepiness. Forty percent (two out of five) regularly go to bed after 11:00 p.m. on school nights. Busy schedules, late nights, and early school starting times conspire to make teenagers chronically sleepy. Being tired reduces our tolerance of stress. It leaves us less energy to deal with the thoughts and emotions stress can trigger. The U.S. National Institutes

The Dangers of Sleepiness

The National Highway Traffic and Safety Administration estimates that drowsy driving, most likely caused by not getting enough sleep, causes over 100,000 motor vehicle accidents each year, resulting in some 40,000 injuries and 1,550 deaths annually.

of Health determined through a variety of studies that teenagers, on average, need 8.5 to 9.25 hours of sleep per night to function their best.

How much sleep do you get each night?

4. Get some exercise.

Physical activity of just about any kind, even in moderation, can improve our health and well-being. A little exercise is better than no exercise at all! Health recommendations for exercise are not as strenuous as you might think. The U.S. Department of Health and Human Services suggests aiming to accumulate at least thirty minutes (adults) or sixty minutes (children) of moderate physical activity most days of the week, preferably daily. Moderate physical activity is defined as any activity that requires as much energy as it would take to walk two miles in thirty minutes. No matter what activity you choose, you can do it all at once, or spread it out over two or three times during the day. Try walking or riding a bike to a friend's house instead of riding in a car. Or take the stairs whenever you can rather than using an elevator or escalator. Instead of letting the dog out into a fenced backyard, take him for a walk around the block. Just get up and move!

Balancing Act

Physical exercise can also be a great way to vent emotions caused by stress. Take up running or kick-boxing or swimming—anything that allows you to express yourself physically in a safe way. Most experts agree regular exercise is key to managing stress.

5. Practice stress-reduction exercises

Stretch your muscles and use deep breathing techniques (see page 110), put yourself in a calming environment (recline in a quiet room, take a bath, soak in a hot tub,

Physical activity is a healthy way to vent tension.

Exercise Equals

The Nicholas Institute of Sports Medicine and Athletic Trauma estimates that the following activities use roughly the same amount of energy (calories):

- walking two miles in thirty minutes
- playing ninety minutes of golf (without carts)
- climbing stairs for twenty minutes
- downhill skiing for forty minutes
- raking leaves for an hour
- shoveling snow for approximately eighteen minutes
- riding a stationary bike for twenty minutes

play soft music, or get a massage). All these actions can reduce the physical side effects of stress by lowering our heart rates and slowing our breathing. As we physically begin to relax, we can more effectively handle stress mentally and emotionally.

Mentally Handling Stress

1. Keep things in perspective. Be realistic.

Don't turn tigers into pussycats or pussycats into tigers. Look at things as they really are. Then you're better prepared to deal with the circumstances. Also remember that nobody's perfect; give yourself permission to make a mistake now and then. You won't be able to please every-

Balancing Act

> ### Try This Deep Breathing Exercise!
>
> Sit comfortably in a chair, on the floor, or on your bed. Sit up straight, close your eyes, and allow your hands and arms to hang naturally at your sides. Now begin to take a slow, deep breath in through your nose. As you inhale, slowly raise your hands and arms toward the ceiling, timing the peak of your breath (the deepest part of your inhale) with your farthest reach (when your hands are as far above your head as they can go). Then slowly exhale through your mouth and allow your hands and arms to slowly drop again to your sides.
>
> Repeat two or three times. You'll feel more relaxed almost immediately!

one all the time, nor should you have to. You can only do your best.

2. Tell yourself the truth, the whole truth, and nothing but the truth.

Some wise person once said, "you can't prevent birds from flying over your head, but you can keep them from making a nest in your hair." It's the same way with thoughts. We can't keep thoughts from popping into our heads, but we can keep them from making us believe

Taking time to relax is an important stress-management technique.

things that aren't true. Step back from your emotions, and weigh your thoughts honestly and accurately as they enter your mind. Is what you're thinking exaggerated? Is it minimized? Is it one side of the story? Is it only half true? Or is it the complete, accurate picture? Do what you can to keep your thinking objective and true.

3. Stop snowballs before they roll away.

We've all experienced the fury of snowballing thoughts and emotions. We think one thought, which leads to another, which leads to then another. Like the childhood game of "telephone" or "gossip," the final thought at the end of the line barely resembles the thought that started the process.

Instead, it might look something like this: You see your boyfriend, Troy, whispering in your best friend's ear. You might think, *Troy is talking to Janet. I wonder what he's saying. They're standing awfully close over there. I'll bet he likes her. I'll bet he likes her even more than he likes me. He's just using me to get to her. He's probably telling her he wants to go out with her. He's planning to dump me. . . .*

By the end of these snowballing thoughts, you've lost your boyfriend, Janet is a backstabbing friend, and Troy is an unfaithful jerk—all because of runaway thoughts that weren't even true. In this situation, Troy was planning a surprise party for you, and his whispered comment was nothing more than a request for Janet to help him plan the surprise!

We've all fallen prey to this kind of thinking, and the place to stop this process is when the first thought enters our minds. At that point, it's only a tiny snowball we can keep from rolling—but if we let it go unchecked, it can become a roaring avalanche.

4. Be optimistic and thankful.

Look for the positive, instead of the negative. Attitude can have a huge impact on our ability to handle stress. What can you be thankful for in this situation? What possible good can come from these events? Maybe the only good in this circumstance is that you're learning to handle pressure, but that is a *good* thing (even though it may not feel like it at the time). Or perhaps the only other good thing is that one day you'll be able to help someone

Many people find that yoga helps them handle stress better emotionally, intellectually, and physically.

else who has gone through the same or a similar thing. Be assured of this: no difficulty is ever one hundred per-cent bad; something good can always come out of it, even if it's nothing more than learning to manage pain.

5. Ask what, not why?

Instead of moaning, "Why me?" ask yourself, "What can I learn from this?" Begin to view stressful situations as opportunities to grow and learn in ways you never could have had you not experienced the stress. Sometimes we need to learn things about ourselves. Sometimes we need to learn things about others. Sometimes we need to learn something basic, like how to accept things we can't change. Whatever your stressor, try to treat it as a chance to learn something new.

Emotionally Handling Stress

1. Make friends.

Find someone with whom you can talk about your prob-lems, someone with whom you can be yourself without being afraid of ridicule. Having someone to support us, give us advice, or just listen can go a long way toward helping us handle our stress.

2. Cry if you have to.

In other words, allow yourself to feel, then vent appropri-ately (in a way that won't harm you or another person). Cry. Take a walk. Punch a pillow. Pet your dog. Go for a run. Write in a journal. Make up a song. Paint a picture. Do whatever allows you to express your feelings in a constructive way.

3. Don't do more than you can or want to do.

When we find ourselves doing too much, we may break commitments and let people down. That makes us feel even more stressed-out and worse about ourselves. If you're too busy to fulfill your commitments, cut an activity or two. Which things are you doing because you really want to be involved in them, and which are you doing to please or satisfy others? Decide what's most important to you, or what you most enjoy, and keep those activities. Cut something else. Remember, as you think about your schedule, emotional health requires "down time"—time when we have nothing scheduled and nothing to do. How much "down time" is in your schedule this week? Is there enough? What can you do about it?

4. Remember, you have more control than you think.

Similar to the "Just Say No" anti-drug campaign, remember that you can "just say no" to other things more often than you think. You can say "no" to being treated poorly by friends (find new friends). You can say "no" to a bad job situation (change jobs). You can say "no" to being bad-mouthed by your boyfriend (walk away from the relationship). You can say "no" to never getting enough sleep (cut back on some activities or work hours). You can say "no" to negative, self-put-down thoughts (replace them with positive thoughts). You really can say "no" to invitations to do things you really don't want or think you should do (just decline to participate). You can say "no."

Balancing Act

When people work together, stress may not seem so great.

Of course, some things in life we can't decline: the death of a loved one or pet, an accident or injury, a bad report from the doctor, a chronic illness or disability, a family's move to a new neighborhood, our parents' marriage problems or divorce. In these situations, though we can't control the stress of the circumstances, we can control our responses to the stress. By accepting that there are things in this life we can't control, and working to control *our responses* to these things (by using the tips in this chapter), we're doing the best we can do, and it should be enough.

5. Don't overlook religion and spiritual advisors.

People who pray stay healthier and handle stress more effectively. At least that's what doctors are beginning to suspect. So much so, in fact, that the U.S. National Institutes of Health is funding a five-year study to see if prayer intervention can improve the health of cancer patients. The study, which began in 2000, is being conducted by Dr. Diane Becker of Johns Hopkins University and Dr. Harold G. Koenig of Duke University, an associate professor of medicine and psychiatry who has studied the effects of religion on health for over fifteen years. Prayer seems to help people in many ways.

As one researcher concluded after examining several studies on the relationship between faith and handling stress, ". . . it seems that religion and faith can play an important role in the amount of stress in a person's life and the way they choose to cope with it. Faith gives a person a place to find support personally through a relationship with God, but it is also a place to find social support from others with similar beliefs."

So make time to practice your religion. Meet with your pastor, priest, rabbi, or other spiritual guide. Talk with a trusted confidant or **mentor** who shares your beliefs and can encourage you. You can also cope with stress by deepening your spirituality through prayer or meditation.

Stress. It can be good or bad, helpful or harmful, life-giving or life-draining. How we handle it makes all the difference. Think of all the sources of stress in your life. How are you handling them? Can you cope? What one thing can you do this week, or what one change can you make to handle your stress in a healthy, productive way? Try it and see what happens.

Carlson, Dale and Hannah Carlson. *Where's Your Head: Psychology for Teens.* Madison, Conn.: Bick, 1998.

Carlson, Richard. *Don't Sweat the Small Stuff for Teens: Simple Ways to Keep Your Cool in Stressful Times.* New York: Hyperion, 2000.

Egeberg, Gary. *My Feelings Are Like Wild Animals: How Do I Tame Them?: A Practical Guide to Help Teens (And Former Teens) Feel and Deal with Painful Emotions.* Mahwah, N.J.: Paulist Press, 1998.

Espeland, Pamela. *Life Lists for Teens: Tips, Steps, Hints, and How-Tos for Growing Up, Getting Along, Learning, and Having Fun.* Minneapolis, Minn.: Free Spirit Publishing, 2003.

Hipp, Earl. *Fighting Invisible Tigers: A Stress Management Guide for Teens.* Minneapolis, Minn.: Free Spirit Publishing, 1995.

McGraw, Jay. *Life Strategies for Teens.* New York: Fireside, 2000.

McGraw, Jay. *Life Strategies for Teens Workbook.* New York: Fireside, 2001.

Powell, Mark and Kelly Adams. *Stress Relief: The Ultimate Teen Guide.* Lanham, Mass.: Rowman and Littlefield, 2003.

Rutledge, Jill Zimmerman. *Dealing with the Stuff That Makes Life Tough: The 10 Things That Stress Teen Girls Out and How to Cope with Them.* St. Louis, Mo.: McGraw-Hill/Contemporary Books, 2003.

Sapolsky, Robert M. *Why Zebras Don't Get Ulcers: A Guide to Stress, Stress-Related Diseases, and Coping.* New York: Freeman, 1994.

Seaward, Brian and Linda Bartlett. *Hot Stones and Funny Bones: Teens Helping Teens Cope with Stress and Anger.* Deerfield Beach, Fla.: Health Communications, 2002.

Sluke, Sara Jane and Vanessa Torres. *The Complete Idiot's Guide® to Dealing with Stress for Teens.* Indianapolis, Ind.: Alpha Books, 2001.

Youngs, Bettie and Jennifer Youngs. *A Taste-Berry Teen's Guide to Managing the Stress and Pressures of Life.* Deerfield Beach, Fla.: Health Communications, 2001.

Weston, Carol. *For Teens Only: Quotes, Notes, and Advice You Can Use.* New York: HarperTrophy, 2002.

A.N.S.W.E.R. (Adolescents Never Suicide When Everyone Responds)
Mental Health Association of the Heartland
739 Minnesota Avenue
Kansas City, KS 66101
(913) 281-2221, Ext. 130
www.teenanswer.org/

Anxiety Disorders Association of America
8730 Georgia Avenue, Suite 600
Silver Spring, MD 20910
(240) 485-1001
www.adaa.org/

American Foundation for Suicide Prevention's Youth Suicide Prevention Campaign
American Foundation for Suicide Prevention (AFSP)
120 Wall Street, 22nd Floor
New York, New York 10005
(212) 363-3500 or toll free: (888) 333-AFSP
www.afsp.org/education/teen/

Focus Adolescent Services (on Stress)
www.focusas.com/Stress.html

Freedom From Fear
308 Seaview Ave.
Staten Island, New York 10305
(718) 351-1717
www.freedomfromfear.org/

Health Finder
U.S. Department of Health and Human Services
Office of Disease Prevention and Health Promotion

Office of Public Health and Science,
Office of the Secretary
200 Independence Avenue SW., Room 738G
Washington, DC 20201
(202) 205-8611
www.healthfinder.gov/

High School Hub
(on-line academic help for high school students)
highschoolhub.org/hub/hub.cfm

Kidzworld Media (Canada)
Suite 612
475 Howe Street
Vancouver, British Columbia
Canada V6C 2B3
(604) 688-2010 or toll free: (800) 668-0071

Kidzworld Media (United States)
c/o Suite 260
6121 Lakeside Drive
Reno, Nevada 89511

National Foundation for Abused and Neglected
Children (N.F.A.N.C.)
P.O. Box 1841
Chicago, Illinois 60690-1841
www.gangfreekids.org/

The Nemours Foundation: Teens Health Answers and
Advice
www.kidshealth.org/teen/

The Open Diary
www.opendiary.com/

Puberty101.com
www.puberty101.com/

The Stress Management Institute
aboutstress.com/

TeenCentre.net
www.teencentre.net/

Thinkquest: Teens and Stress
library.thinkquest.org/13561/english/

Tools for Coping Series
A Public Service of James J. Messina, Ph.D. & Constance
M. Messina, Ph.D.
6319 Chauncy Street
Tampa, FL 33647
www.coping.org/

Xanga.com: The WebLog Community
www.xanga.com/

Publisher's note:
The Web sites listed on these pages were active at the time of publication. The publisher is not responsible for Web sites that have changed their addresses or discontinued operation since the date of publication. The publisher will review and update the Web sites upon each reprint.

acute Characterized by severity, critical.

central nervous system All parts of the brain and spinal cord.

cerebral palsy A physical disability caused by damage to the brain either before or during birth and often manifested by speech disturbances or lack of muscular coordination.

chronic Always present, having frequent recurrence, long duration.

coping mechanism Something that helps one deal with or overcome a problem or negative situation.

Ecstasy An illegal drug that alters the emotions and can cause an individual to lose rational thought and self-control.

epilepsy A disorder caused by disturbed electrical impulses in the brain and often manifested by convulsive episodes.

hormones Substances produced by cells and that travel via the bloodstream and have an effect on physiological activity (such as growth).

irate Incensed, angry.

lethargic Sluggish, inactive.

mental health professionals People such as psychiatrists, psychiatric nurses, and clinical sociologists, who have studied and obtained the degrees and licenses legally necessary to provide medical assistance to individuals with mental health needs.

mentor A trusted person who provides advice, guidance, and education.

metabolism The total chemical changes that occur in living cells by which energy is provided for vital processes and activities.

nonchalance Casual indifference, lack of concern.

overachieving perfectionist A person whose goal is to always perform at the highest level and achieve more than is normally expected.

perceive Become aware of, to interpret based on one's senses and observations.

progressive Advancing, increasing in severity.

rehab Short for rehabilitation, such as physical therapy necessary to restore disabled parts of the body to maximum capability.

SARS Severe Acute Respiratory Syndrome; a respiratory illness caused by a coronavirus; characterized by high fever, body aches, dry cough, and pneumonia; first reported in Asia in 2003 and then quickly spread to more than two dozen countries.

STD A sexually transmitted disease such as AIDS, gonorrhea, syphilis, and herpes.

suppressed Subdued, held back, hidden.

INDEX

PICTURE CREDITS

Joan Esherick is a full-time author, freelance writer, and professional speaker who lives outside of Philadelphia, Pennsylvania, with her husband, three teenagers, and black Labrador retriever named Baxter. She is the author of thirteen books, including *Our Mighty Fortress: Finding Refuge in God* (Moody Press, 2002), *The Big Picture: The Bible's Story in Thirty Short Scenes*, and multiple books with Mason Crest Publishers. Joan has contributed dozens of articles to national print periodicals and speaks nationwide. For more information about her, you can visit her Web site at www.joanesherick.com.

Dr. Bridgemohan is an instructor in pediatrics at Harvard Medical School and is a Board Certified Developmental-Behavioral Pediatrician on staff in the Developmental Medicine Center at Children's Hospital, Boston. She specializes in assessment and treatment of autism and developmental disorders in young children. Her clinical practice includes children and youth with autism, hearing impairment, developmental language disorders, global delays, mental retardation, and attention and learning disorders. Dr. Bridgemohan is coeditor of "Bright Futures: Case Studies for Primary Care Clinicians: Child Development and Behavior," a curriculum used nationwide in pediatric residency training programs.

Dr. Sara Forman graduated from Barnard College and Harvard Medical School. She completed her residency in Pediatrics at Children's Hospital of Philadelphia and a fellowship in Adolescent Medicine at Children's Hospital Boston (CHB). She currently is an attending in Adolescent Medicine at CHB, where she has served as Director of the Adolescent Outpatient Eating Disorders Program for the past nine years. She has also consulted for the National Eating Disorder Screening Project on its high school initiative and has presented at many conferences about teens and eating disorders. In addition to her clinical and administrative roles in the Eating Disorders Program, Dr. Forman teaches medical students and residents and coordinates the Adolescent Medicine rotation at CHB. Dr. Forman sees primary care adolescent patients in the Adolescent Clinic at CHB, at Bentley College, and at the Germaine Lawrence School, a residential school for emotionally disturbed teenage girls.